# Anatomy of a soul

C000131954

## ~Rainbows~

Drops of rain pouring slowly

Like silver tears of the sky;

What a sight, it is both light and gloomy,

Both sadness and smiles.

Rainbows enlivening this greedy world,

Fissures turning slowly to gold;

The soldier of sun and rain and lightning bolt:

The rainbow is happiness' sword.

# ~Impale~

Impale me, I await

Impale me with lies,

Hang me with pain.

Kneel and hit

I am at your feet,

As I receive

Your love that hurts more than being killed

By a bloody guillotine.

## ~Eden~

When I look at you,

All I feel is sparks:

I am lost in your smile,

I am lost in your eyes.


Sweet is the call of perdition,

I drink in your words

For you are my world,

Your smile is my religion.


Am I from heaven?

Are you from hell?

I'll give up my Eden

For I am under your spell.

## ~Ancient Treasures~

There are songs as old as time

Lost in years, wiped in rain.

Stories as many as stars on the sky,

Forever disappearing in a clepsydrical hurricane.


Cry old soul, for this is true:

Fortunes are lost, treasures are gone.

It is our fault, for we are prone

To banish and vanish all that is pure.

## ~Sweet pain~

There are no gods.

No divinity. No grace.

Celestial prayers, all in vain…

There are no gods; Only pain.

## ~Kindness is the purest beauty~

Kindness is an underrated beauty,

For nothing glows brighter than a kind heart,

When the world pushes away all but the mad

Kindness is the one to stand its ground.


Kind souls, happy faces,

Sweet people, sweet phrases,

Embrace of golden smiles,

In their eyes you can see the sun shining bright.

## ~Aren't we all~

Aren't we all just little drops

In the oceans full of rain,

So small, so many, yet never perfect at all?


We're just little fragments of dust,

Just pieces of reddish rust,

With the remembrance of the past,

When we hoped for something good, at last.


Aren't we all

Just another lock at the door,

Always used and always carried

At the hands of so many.


Life is dull, I wonder why

Sometimes do we even try

To make something out of it,

When we all share the same ending.

*~But birds are free, unlike you sweetheart~*

What if I was a bird,

Flying towards the burning sun, the sky,

A phoenix rising in its rebirth,

Fire on my wings, lullaby in my flight.

## ~Angels~

Angels in their bright light

Have keen from heaven

Have lightened the night;

Their sweet voices,

Their holy symphony

Have left traces

Of pure harmony.

Soon their eyes cried in gold,

Their faces pale, cold as stone,

Their hair of fire, pious sin

They had silver on their skin.

No one breathed,

No one blinked,

For all knew what this meant,

Angels surround us, heaven broke,

They all kneeled; For this is the end.

## ~Unknown~

Don't mesmerize my heart in fear of the unknown,

I've got a myriad of questions, deep within my soul.

Some are concealed in silver, some in gold,

Some are forbidden, foreign, untold.

What lies whenever we whisper the truth,

For a lie is a lie unless you hide it from the world.

Answer my cries; there is a key to the chamber

Of the foreign truth, by the world forgotten.

Do not voice it; I wish not to know,

Some secrets are better left unknown.

## ~Woe~

In dust we crumble one by one,
We feel destruction in our bones,
We burn like the sun in the sky,
We turn to ashes; we turn to stones.

The gods feast in our woe
They dine for our misery;
There is no way out of sough,
We are the world's forgotten tragedy.

*~It must be me~*

Up in the clouds

The goddess laughs-

Silly humans, crippled souls,

Shells of sins, haunted world,

Foolish humans,

No way to carry on.

Up in the clouds, the goddess laughs-

They wished for rain,

Now sink in the flood.

*~Once upon a lie~*

You once promised you will give me

The moon, the sun, the stars;

What you never understood was

All I wanted was a place in your heart…

But those were lies, now I know,

That you never loved me back.

Step by step, wish by wish,
The darkest shade of desire
The dreams created just to perish
Into the flames of hellfire.

Flowers gloom, flowers grow,
In the moonlight, the unknown,
The stars sublime, gold to rust,
Everything turned to dust.

Dust as empty dreams at night
Dreaming at the pale moonlight.
Darkest glow, foreign sin,
And the silence of a scream.

## ~Elysium~

Don't you despair,

Our souls are alive,

Even though from life we fell.

We'll swim in Styx

We'll get lost in mist

Our stories are far from the end.

Let's run to the island

The island of the blessed,

Away from all we know,

We can finally be ourselves.

We'll get lost in Elysium,

Where Pindar, Hesiod, Homer,

They'll write about our lives,

How mystical they were.

Broken souls turned to ashes
So many hearts by pain crashed,
Turning down the misery
To the greatest mystery.

Hearts as light as a feather,
The feelings more changeable now than ever,
Rain flooding all their senses,
The thunder leaving them defenseless.

Scattered dreams, wishes that failed
Wounds opened up again,
Opportunities lost and restrained
Joy lost in the ocean of pain.

## ~We all fell from grace~

You sweep for beauty, tremble at grace?

Oh darling, pray I tell:

Beauty is a shallow, terrific debt

Grace is rough, tangles the phase

Of a lusty creation of mess.

Beauty is all nothing but a nightmare

Of dreams lost in disgrace.

*~But heaven is no greater than fire and earth~*

Call me by my name as you hold my hand,

All of the reality perishes, we are made of heaven:

Celestial sinners, dressed in gold

Sang by the Earth's most rotten folk.

Lust, what is lust?

What's lust remained when all is lost?

Lust, a craving from the pit,

A wish of madness, why indeed!

Away! Away, might we all pray,

Pray of mercy, pray of sins,

Pray of the darkness from the abyss.

Away- What's lust?

The passion of unarmed fury. At what cost?

Away! Lost. I am lost.

I lusted my way out of the chaos.

## ~All is lost~

The sense is lacking nowadays

All you see are just dazed faces.

Empty souls, empty heads,

Bodies without spirits.

Hope is gone-

Long live destruction!

No one can protect us all

From what is yet to come;

We lost the sense,

We lost ourselves,

Empty souls, empty heads;

Here comes the end.

## ~Mother Moon~

Mother Moon, holy goddess

Forget my flaws, erase my felonies,

For I have failed, pathos in darkness,

For I am my own nemesis.


Mother Moon, to you I pray,

I am your disciple, I am your apprentice,

I kneel to you, and I obey,

Please, Goddess Moon, forgive my sins.

## ~Antique Desire~

Silver stars shining upon,
Silver memories rising on
Barely dreamt waves of gold,
Fantasies from ancestries foretold.

## ~Once upon a dishonest love~

Do you remember, a long time ago,

You said you love me from within your soul.

I took your word, said I love you too,

We drowned in a love too good to be true.


Once upon a time,

You took me by my hand:

No lie hidden, no truth unsaid;

I was yours. You were mine.


Once upon a story, long time ago,

I said I loved you from within my soul.

You took my word, said you love me too,

But both of us knew, none of this was true.

## *~Maybe one day~*

See? Have I not said,

That in the end they'll turn away?

Foolish heart, once again,

You thought that they would remain?

Wipe your tears, ease your pain?

Oh, my foolish heart,

Friends always remain behind.

## ~We loved~

We loved with fire,

We burned in passion,

The flames have danced

In our destruction.


We loved from beneath the stars,

Eyes full of wonder, hearts open wide,

We drank from golden crystals,

We loved the dark, we loved the light.

*~Fight for peace, die for freedom~*

War is near,

Hold your sword tight,

It would be a long fight.

War is near,

Do not give up.

Blood shall be shed tonight.

What can I say, that hasn't been said?

What can I do, that hasn't been done?

I cannot take the warmness of the sun,

I cannot steal the light of a day.


What is left to think?

What is left to write?

The world sold out its grip

Of the creation under our sight.


What can I see, such as no one has seen?

Can I touch the matter with my skin?

I wish I can have what everyone has,

Things I know I cannot have.


I wish for a reviewed point of view

Forgotten wonders waiting for their muse.

I wish for the world as it has survived,

The simplicity of a raw midnight.


The paradise still not wondered,

The dreams yet to be discovered:

The moon, the sun, the wild

The stars glowing up in the sky.

What can I have?

The world, the Earth,

The freedom of a flying bird?

The smiles, the dreams, the sky,

If only I opened my wings to fly…

This is who I am

I will not crumble.

I will not fall.

This is my heart,

This is my soul.

I will not die.

I will not fail.

I have to fight destruction,

I have to fight pain.

# ~Memory~

I remember, when I was a kid

I used to think

That one day the world will crumble at my feet.

But now I know,

In order to succeed,

Sacrifice the ones that need

You by their side.

This is a matter of death and life;

The world shall crumble, not at my feet,

But at the crimes that I commit.

## ~Consequences~

Don't beg for rain,

If you cannot stand in mud.

Don't destroy a soul,

If you cannot wipe away its blood.

# ~Masquerade~

Masquerade,

So many faces hidden under silky masks.

Masquerade,

So many secrets hidden in their eyes.

Masquerade,

So many smiles faked in their dance.

Masquerade,

So many truths untold by their lies.


Carry on, waltz all night,

Only they know the madness created;

The darkness taking over their mind

The tears that are in silver graved.

## ~All is lost~

The sense is lacking nowadays

All you see are just dazed faces.

Empty souls, empty heads,

Bodies without spirits.

Hope is gone-

Long live destruction!

No one can protect us all

From what is yet to come;

We lost the sense,

We lost ourselves,

Empty souls, empty heads;

Here comes the end.

Curse the curse of the folk,

On this very rigid spot!

Curse the heavens! Curse you, world!

Curse my spirit, curse my soul;

Curse me. I have been cursed,

Cursed by this condemned world…

Mighty dreams, my wishes have come true!

Rusty stains of virtue-

Rambling oceans, may all sweep

Sink the oceans in my dream

Dry worlds, chaos most indeed,

Pry madness, crimes of the deed

Let the oceans of sin

Sink in the madness underneath.

## ~Murder~

We murdered our essence

Look behind, all is lost,

The present with its presence

Sacrificed the world we knew.

All is left is what we make,

All becomes what we have speared.

No glance behind, how can it be?

We murdered who we used to be.

## ~Angel of Death~

You asked me: why does the night's wind always blow?

As if I am supposed to know

As if I am the wind that blows,

As if I am the wind that blows.


Why do the stars always shine bright?

You asked softly last midnight.

I beg, "How can I possibly know that?"

You smiled, "For you are the brightest star."


I wondered how were you supposed to know

That is not the wind that blows

In the middle of the night,

It is my whisper in the dark.


And may you never figure out

I am not the brightest star;

I am merely a dream

That people have when they give

Away their very last breath.

*~Because we are all fading away~*

And often, might we ask
Why do we let our souls fall apart?
Why do we let the sorrow of the past
Take away the present way too fast,
Turning our existence to remains of ash.

## ~Lie to me~

Lie to me,

You do it so well

Is lying an art?

You'll be its master.

Lie to me, do it again

Oh that, how I love,

Whenever you lie,

I tend to believe.

## ~Little bird~

Little bird trying to fly
For the very first time.
But does it even know,
One can never let go?

The wind, the rain, the thunder's sound
Will try to push you into the ground.
Little bird, always know,
You shall never let go.

And if you do, then say goodbye
To your freedom, to the sky,
Embrace the dark and carry on,
Your wings will perish in the cold.

## ~Gone~

So, what if you're away?

The rainbow still rises after the rain,

The sea still waves its velvet skin,

The birds still fly, the fish still swim.


So, what if you're not coming back?

The sun will still shine bright,

The moon won't stop glowing at night,

There will still be darkness behind the light.


You're gone. But, so what?

Am I supposed to cry all night?

To pray, to beg so you'll come back?

Oh, darling, I do not need you in my life.

## ~Hold on tight, here comes the night~

When the world will crush down

No one will be left standing,

Soul for soul, one for one,

Faith is forbidden. Faith is gone.


No one left to shed the tears,

Celestial holiness transfigured to rotten greed.

What's left of us? No hope, no will;

Outside the world in madness is crumbling…

*~Your mask~*

Sing me your mind,

Write me your soul,

Your scarring thoughts,

Your sacred glow.


Share me your story,

All the terrors, all the glory;

I want to know the real you,

Not the shell you pretend is true.


What makes you smile,

What makes you cry?

Which thoughts keep you up at night?

Which songs are harmonies to your heart?


Love is not easy, love is blind,

It fades your mind, it chants your heart,

It crumbles deep within your soul,

As sweet as the wisdom of ancient songs.


Sing me your defined lullaby,

Show me the stars under the sky;

Electric eyes, sound of woe,

Electric eyes, unedged soul.

Let me know the real you,

The 'you' you are only with you.

For who am I to love a mask,

Placed to hide you from your past?

Her grave has flowers all around,

They make it seem so light,

They remind me of her smile,

Her smile, innocent and bright.


They said that sometimes you can hear her,

She sings her song trough the birds,

Her song is sweet, full of love,

She sings of wonder; she sings of life.


Yet I was deaf of her sound,

I was blind to her beauty.

Now I can finally see:

The birds sing. The flowers bloom.

She is happy now, for she is alone.

## ~Eclipse~

When the world crushes
Where would you stand?
Will you choose me,
Or will you choose them?

You have to pick a side,
It is life or death.
Will you die with them,
Or will you fight with me?

There is nowhere to run, there is no way to hide.
The time is up, tonight we fight.
You are with them… I see, you choose light,
Darling, don't you know?
What is in the darkness, will burn you alive.

*~I am the one you need to be saved from~*

Who said I need to be saved?

I am not a fragile flower

Hid in a thorny heather;

I am not a candle

Melting, wax on my skin,

I am the fire

Burning from within.

I am not a flower,

But the most pungent thorn.

## ~Running~

I run,

Through the darkest of forests,

Hair on my face, scratches on my back.

I sprint without rest,

No time to look back.


I run, for this is the only way,

I run without looking away.

The past is here, catching me,

No matter how much I run,

I can never outrun it.

The past is here:

It will never set me free.

## ~If I'm gone~

If I am gone,

Who will remember me?

Who will sing my memory?

Who will follow me away,

Who will run and who will stay?


Who will search for any hint

To my sacred rhapsody?

Who will find me when they dream,

Followed by sublimity?


When I am gone, if I am gone,

Will I be gone?

Where will I be, what will I be?

A bird flying freely in the wind?

Or will I be just ground and stone?


For if I am gone

I will search for you:

The freedom calling me my name:

Until the end, there you stood,

Smiling, reaching for my hand;

If I am gone, I'm gone with you

## ~Love is a crime~

Is loving a crime?
For all I loved,
Now is gone.
Tempted I consider
That is but my fault,
For all I loved and all I love,
Disappears without a sign.
Love is a crime, for it kills
Hearts only with a kiss.

*~If only we were brave enough~*

The world is tearing dreams apart,

Madness is prying for your heart;

Lose the way you'd never found

Lost our minds, forever we run…

## ~We're a tragedy~

We look like a tragedy,

Don't you agree?

There is something antic about us,

We came from myths;

We're one with the muses,

We're one with the sea.

In your eyes I see

Sweet Dionysus staring back at me.

But we're lost in madness,

We are a tragedy.

We're drunk in ambrosia,

We're lost in the myths.

## ~Sin as you sin~

Sin as you sin,

Regret after regret,

This never-ending sunset

Holding to your debt.


Sin as you sin,

Your eyes blinking tears,

Fire in your daydreams

Burning you piece by piece.


The puzzle is undone,

The pieces dance with flames;

The world seems to crush down,

Scattering in your hands.


So, sin as you sin,

Your heart will hold on as long as it takes,

But how much do you think

You can outrun your fate?

*~Darling, no one can save this broken world~*

Her eyes have seen the end

Replaying all over again

She is terrified by everything that has yet to come.


She screams for help but it is undone

And what can be done, when all is lost?

We fight and fight, but for what cost?


She holds the key to the untold,

She holds the key deep within her soul.

*~But I was born when the spirits were lost~*

Damn my heart, how it longs

For adventures and foreign odds,

Tragedies as in Greek myths,

Astonishing madness lost in the labyrinth…

## ~Power is desire, do not deny~

Sweet is the taste of power.

Some say is sour, some taste salt,

But power is as sweet as an innocent deed,

Honey, soft hands, fire in veins.

What is power?

Is what we call when life finally

Tastes as a sinful tragedy on sacrificed smiles;

Power is you, sweet soul, corrupted grin.

Power we feel when we are close to win.

*~May them perish~*

No salvation. None remained.

Cry for yourself, cry in pain,

The sky has crushed, the end is here.

Nowhere to hide, try not to scream.

Close your eyes, hold on tight,

Only one survives the night.

## ~You~

I've dreamed of foreign fairytales,

In a storm of wonder, there was you:

The light illuminating your face;

For that I knew, it was but a dream

It was too right to be true.

## ~Sweet girl~

Sweet girl, do not shade your tears
Do not let them ruin your dreams.
Who are they to condemn you?
Who are they to control you?

Oh, sweet girl, just run away,
From the past and from the pain
Life gives you hope and faith and trust,
Don't let them turn it to dust,
To protect them is a must.

My most sweet girl, ready to flee
From the cold breeze of wild wind
Sand storms may shatter her bones.
Break her heart, turn it to stone.

Run sweet girl, don't you look back,
They are no longer your pack.
The she-wolf will sleep alone tonight,
Sweet girl flying out of sight.

*~And for that I am grateful~*

Oh no, no we do not belong,

We are lost, by madness found;

Sweet harmonies, purified sounds,

Oh, sweet darkness, we do not belong.

# Contents

Printed in Great Britain
by Amazon